WASHINGTON

PHOTOGRAPHY BY JOHN MARSHALL

TEXT BY RUTH KIRK

GRAPHIC ARTS CENTER PUBLISHING COMPANY, PORTLAND, OREGON

International Standard Book Number 0-932575-64-1
Library of Congress Catalog Number 88-80536
© MCMLXXXVIII by Graphic Arts Center Publishing Company
P.O. Box 10306 • Portland, Oregon 97210 • 503/226-2402
Editor-in-Chief • Douglas A. Pfeiffer
Associate Editor • Jean Andrews
Designer • Robert Reynolds
Cartography • Tom Patterson and Manoa Mapworks
Typographer • Paul O. Giesey/Adcrafters
Color Separations • Graphic Color
Printer • Dynagraphics, Inc.
Bindery • Lincoln & Allen
Printed in the United States of America

■*Frontispiece:* Rhododendrun with young western hemlock tree
■*Title Page:* Mount Rainier from the south

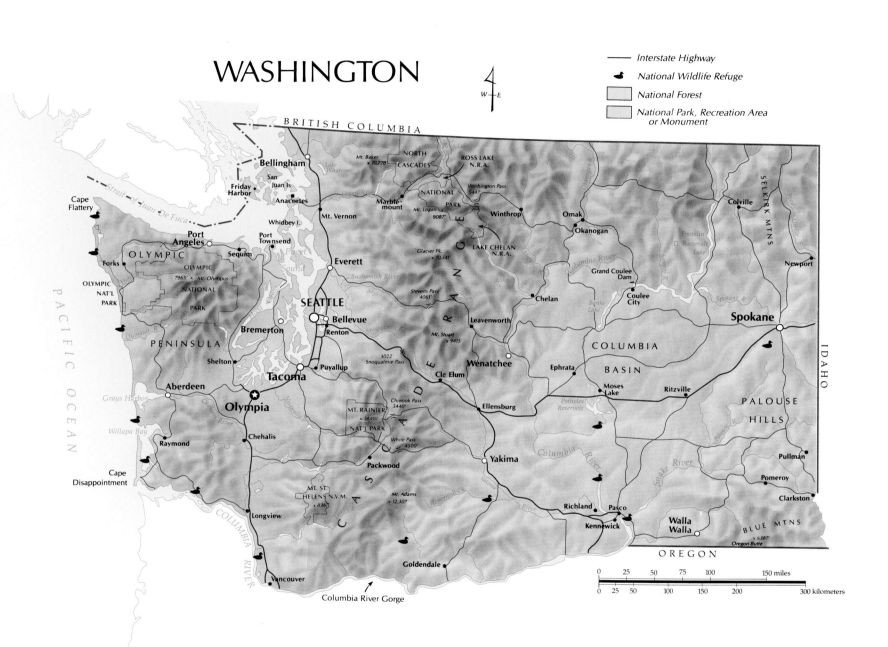

WASHINGTON

W—E

Interstate Highway
National Wildlife Refuge
National Forest
National Park, Recreation Area or Monument

BRITISH COLUMBIA

Cape Flattery

Strait of Juan De Fuca

Bellingham
San Juan Is.
Friday Harbor
Anacortes
Whidbey I.
Mt. Vernon

Mt. Baker x 10,778'
NORTH CASCADES
ROSS LAKE N.R.A.
Washington Pass 5477'
Marble-mount
NATIONAL
Mt. Logan x 908.7'
Winthrop
PARK
Omak
Okanogan
Colville
SELKIRK MTNS

Port Angeles
Sequim
Port Townsend

OLYMPIC
Forks
OLYMPIC 7965' x Mt. Olympus
OLYMPIC NAT'L PARK
NATIONAL

Everett
Snohomish River
Glacier Pk. x 10,541'
LAKE CHELAN N.R.A.
Grand Coulee Dam

Stevens Pass 4061'
Leavenworth
Chelan
Coulee City
Newport

PACIFIC OCEAN

SEATTLE
Bellevue
Bremerton
Renton
PENINSULA
Shelton
Puyallup
Tacoma
Aberdeen
Grays Harbor

Spokane

Mt. Stuart x 9415'
3022' Snoqualmie Pass
Wenatchee
Cle Elum

COLUMBIA BASIN
Ephrata
Moses Lake
Ritzville

PALOUSE HILLS

IDAHO

Olympia
Chehalis
MT. RAINIER x 14,410' NAT'L PARK
Chinook Pass 5440'
White Pass 4500'
Packwood
Ellensburg
Potholes Reservoir

Willapa Bay
Raymond
Cape Disappointment

Longview

CASCADE
MT. ST. HELENS N.V.M. x 8363'
Mt. Adams x 12,307'

Yakima
Columbia River
Richland
Pasco
Kennewick
Walla Walla

Pullman
Pomeroy
Clarkston

Snake River

BLUE MTNS
x 6387' Oregon Butte

COLUMBIA RIVER

Goldendale

Vancouver
Columbia River Gorge

OREGON

0   25   50   75   100   150 miles

0   25   50   100   150   200   300 kilometers

The water reaches fifty fathoms deep between Lummi Island and Orcas Island, with its 2,407-foot Mount Constitution.

WEST SIDE

To me, this is not the "other" Washington mentioned in tourism ads as an oblique reference to Washington, D.C. This is the "right" Washington.

I sit musing aboard our small sloop *Taku*. We are close to the urban throb of today's cities, yet the boat is no more than a tiny dot on a blue-and-green tapestry of sea and forest. By chance, this quiet southern Puget Sound cove where we ride at anchor is near where Lieutenants Peter Puget and William Whidbey camped — in "a perfect deluge of rain" — their second night out from *Discovery,* the ship commanded by the great British mariner, Captain George Vancouver. That was two centuries ago. Puget and Whidbey were aboard open longboats powered by oarsmen. Their task, according to a memo from Vancouver to Puget was to "Survey the Shore."

Two decades later (the length of time my husband Louis and I have lived in Tacoma), fur traders began to crisscross Washington. Three decades after that, Lieutenant Charles Wilkes, of the U.S. Navy, surveyed Puget Sound and recognized its value along a coast with no other even faintly comparable break from San Francisco to Vancouver Island (indeed, no other large indentation except for Gray's Harbor). Wilkes urged sovereignty over these inland waters, a recommendation that contributed to American insistence on the 49th parallel as the boundary between the United States and Canada.

Britain also wanted Puget Sound — wanted the entire territory north of the Columbia — but trade along the coast of what now is British Columbia was the top priority of the Hudson's Bay Company. If necessary, what later became Washington could be sacrificed. Thus, in 1846, mapmakers inked in today's international line.

While sailing, my husband Louis and I have felt the continuity between those beginning days of the state and the present. Our eyes and souls have reveled in broad waterways, tall trees, and snow-capped mountains. Houses intermix, but — from the water — they rarely predominate. Southern Puget Sound permits an illusion of timelessness. Two humpback whales have been reported this summer, although we have not seen them. Our wildlife coup has been a bald eagle, which we watched as it swooped to the water and rose with a silvery salmon clutched in its talons.

A rural quality lingers along the entire western shore of Puget Sound, from Olympia to Port Townsend; and along much of the eastern shore only Seattle's blocky, black, seventy-six-story Columbia Center newly jutting above the horizon breaks the spell. Without it, you would have little inkling of a city's proximity. An evening excursion from Seattle to Blake Island can still include a stroll along grassy shores and pristine beaches frequented by deer, then a salmon dinner prepared and served by Indian people.

Lieutenants Puget and Whidbey met Natives a few miles north of where we now are anchored. The explorers had started to seine a creek mouth for fish but quit when Salish canoes entered the cove. The new arrivals were clearly displeased. The Englishmen moved on before camping.

At La Push and the mouth of the Hoh River, we used to watch men make cedar dugout canoes. That was in the 1960s while Louis was serving as ranger-naturalist at Olympic National Park. Our Quileute Indian friends, Charlie Howeattle and Ted Hudson, roughed out canoe blanks from split-cedar logs using chain saws, then they switched to hand tools. These included a D-adze with a whalebone handle and a blade made from a Hudson's Bay Company trade axe. Result? Canoes to be fitted with outboard motors and used for gillnetting salmon.

The old-time canoemakers are gone, but their descendants in a dozen western Washington tribes carved cedar canoes as part of the 1989 Centennial celebration, using logs obtained through the National Forest Service (and, on the Peninsula, felled by the state Department of Natural Resources, and yarded and delivered by the National Park Service).

Fifty feet long and six feet wide, such vessels plied this state's salt water for millennia. They carried villagers forty in a canoe to potlatches (ceremonial occasions fundamental to Northwest Coast Indian culture) or — two canoes lashed together as a catamaran — they moved families and household goods from one seasonal site to another. Other canoes of various sizes took men onto the open ocean to hunt whales and fur seals and sea otters, and to fish for halibut and salmon. "We were all the time going places in canoes," Ada Markishtum, an aging Makah woman, used to tell me, when I would visit her to take lessons in making cedarbark baskets. "Even we children knew how to sit still." She would reminisce about waiting for favorable wind and tide conditions, then sailing and paddling across the Strait of Juan de Fuca with her grandmother to trade baskets for blankets and other goods at the Hudson's Bay Company in Victoria, British Columbia.

Today's Indian people still travel widely. Last week at the State Capitol, I visited with Makah friends who had driven the nearly two hundred miles from their Neah Bay reservation to Olympia. They had come to officially open an exhibit of early-day photographs. As a prelude, they danced on the gray marble floor of the Capitol rotunda, their drumbeats and songs echoing off the stone walls as an evidence of the welcome new vigor now sweeping Washington's Indian community.

The velvet rope that usually surrounds the golden seal in the middle of the floor had been removed, and there the masked dancers whirled. They wore scarlet "button blankets," which flared dramatically to display cutouts of Thunderbird and Whale and Wolf appliqued in black. Sequins as well as buttons now highlight these figures. Indian people are adaptable. How else could they have survived?

The Olympic Mountains have rimmed the western horizon most of this day, a jumble of peaks not topping 8,000 feet in elevation but with about fifty glaciers whitening their flanks. Replenishment of the ice comes from storm clouds blown in off the Pacific and chilled while sweeping upward. Their

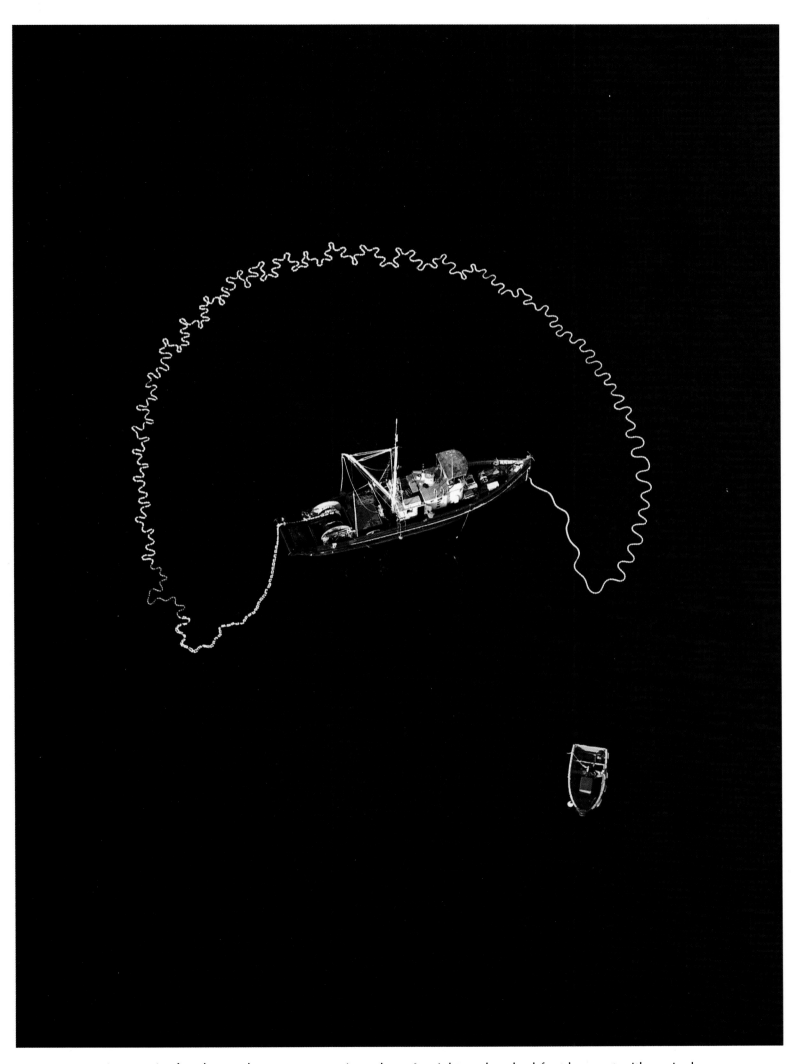

In pursuit of sockeye salmon, a purse seiner closes its eighteen hundred-foot long net with a winch.

Ferry boats thread their way through the one hundred seventy-five named islands of the San Juans.

droplets turn to snow crystals, which fall as a yearly blanket of white. For five years we lived on the Olympic Peninsula, and I still feel that of all the "right" places within this state, the Peninsula just may be the best. Its towns have kept humane scale — perhaps to the regret of their boosters.

Forks and Aberdeen/Hoquiam, on the west side, are hard hit by recent slowdowns in the forest products industry. Their near-term recovery is problematical owing to genuine depletion of trees to cut. Port Townsend, at the northeast tip of the Peninsula, never attained its initial promise. It has had enthusiasm and Victorian mansions, but its downtown buildings have always stayed half empty. The boom began when the tall masts of late 1800s ships lined wharves, and entrepreneurs fostered hope of a link to the transcontinental railroad. But shipping moved on and rails never came.

Sequim now has three stoplights and a constant influx of retirees who come to enjoy the relatively dry weather within the "rain shadow" of the Olympic Mountains. Nearby Port Angeles, largest of the Peninsula's towns, has a population of about 20,000; it takes fifteen minutes to drive kitty-corner across town. For a city interlude, you can board the ferry to Victoria, British Columbia (one and a half hours away), or go to Seattle (two hours by road plus bridge plus ferry).

Two roads and a host of trails lead to the subapline meadows of the Olympics where purple lupine and scarlet paintbrush and golden arnica and a burst of other flowers brighten entire hillsides. Marmots — furry woodchucks utterly engaging to watch — feed on the flowers, sitting on their haunches and pulling the blossoms to their mouths with their forepaws. The marmots tunnel up through snow to begin active life after a winter of hibernation; then curl back underground when fall vegetation scents the air with the aroma of natural silage.

While in the mountains, I always think the high country is my favorite part of the Peninsula. Then we hike the wilderness coast, and I am sure the beach is my primary love. "I've been lazy," reads a note written in my journal a few summers ago while we camped at Point of Arches, the northernmost of the Olympic National Park beaches:

Last night's darkness didn't begin until after 10:30, and it never amounted to much. I slept outside the tent beside a drift log, head toward the jagged near-shore islets and arches that make this beach the most wondrous in the state. Each time I turned, I could check the tide and the night sky's alteration between clouds and stars.

Low tide—a minus 1.4 feet—came at 5:00 a.m. I should have gone with Louis to the tidepools. Instead, at 8:00, the breakfast fire still holds me, its warmth a welcome contrast to the gray chill of the morning. I forgot to bring a macro-lens, and that oversight serves as excuse for laziness. We moderns seem to suffer guilt when we fail to "collect" our experiences.

Aboard *Taku,* I think of the tidepools I should have looked at with eyes, if not camera: water utterly clear, bottoms bejeweled with pink coralline seaweed and jade-green anemones. I think too of a friend who commented on his first look at tidepools as "frightening." I asked what gave him that impression, and he answered: "It's the ruthlessness. A crab or something falls into an anemone and Whomp! That's the end."

Today we rowed ashore and walked paths on Hartstene Island. There, Douglas fir grow two to three feet in diameter, a respectable forest although undoubtedly previously logged. Trees are not a crop "just like corn." We have successfully cut and replanted and cut again, but we will not be able to keep on doing so in the same way. Our existing "harvest" techniques violate too many intricate linkages between organisms.

Western Washington forests renew themselves through small disasters, not wholesale wipeouts. A raging stream pouring rocks and mud down a sidehill or a blowdown toppling a section of forest—even the uprooting of a single tree, which churns the soil and opens the canopy to sunlight—these are the events that perpetuate the green diversity of forests west of the Cascade Mountains. In the stands planted after clear-cutting, sheer density of sapling growth absorbs available light and produces an underlying wasteland of brown needles and infertile shadow.

Furthermore, the "nurselog" trees of the natural forest do more than offer seedlings an elevated perch. They bring a reservoir of nutrients to the forest floor and, in the process of decay, foster the accumulation of still more nutrients. University of Washington forest ecologist Jerry Franklin speaks of a need to manage deadwood as deliberately as has been true of sawlogs. "A tree does all kinds of good things after it dies," he says. "Its ecological role is as great as while it was alive."

Burning debris left from logging, a common practice that turns autumn skies murky, squanders potential. It volatilizes nitrogen in woody tissues and short-circuits a variety of intricate relationships. Regarding fallen trees as "over mature" and useless ignores their after-death role as nurselogs, for down-trees remain an important part of the forest community. What actually happens when a tree falls is this: The trunk is recruited to the forest floor ("recruitment" is a term now used by forest ecologists). Beetles and nematodes and a great host of other organisms soon invade the log and bring with them yeasts and the spores of fungi. These initiate a whole new cycle of nutrient build-up. "There actually are more living cells in a well-rotted log than there were while it stood as part of a living tree," Jerry points out.

Bacteria capable of drawing nitrogen from the air enter through the beetles' galleries. Some of the fungi arriving through those same portals have enzyme systems that decompose a range of complex woody compounds. Some of them produce antibiotics, which suppress certain bacteria. Others give off volatiles that inhibit specific organisms and stimulate others. Certain fungi, thriving only on the roots of living plants, improve their hosts' ability to draw nutrients and moisture from the soil. Hemlock seedlings barely survive until this mutually beneficial relationship is established; their growth depends on the association with fungus.

When you walk beneath trees two hundred feet tall and as much as a thousand years old—or visit the red-cedar grove on Long Island in Willapa Bay, which has been perpetuated without major disturbance for perhaps four thousand years—you are *looking* at more than you are *seeing*. A forest is a community. Trees are one part of the whole.

For millennia, the forest and the water set the stage for human life in this wet west side of Washington. Then newcomers usurped land from Indians and brought a new set of habits and aspirations. Settlement accelerated in the

Haro Strait has been guarded by San Juan Island's Lime Kiln Lighthouse since 1919.

A remodeled turn-of-the-century farmhouse serves guests as a country inn on Orcas Island.

late 1840s, after the boundary issue was settled with England. In both the 1870s and the 1890s, the nation endured financial depressions, partly owing to new industrialization. As if in response, Washingtonians experimented with various reforms, which included half-a-dozen idealistic settlements scattered around Puget Sound.

Best known of these was Home, situated at the cove where I now sit on the bow of *Taku* enjoying the alpenglow on Mount Rainier. Home was a free-spirited community with successive newspapers that espoused "radical" convictions. They printed articles urging that women should be allowed to vote; that religion should not be coerced; and that love between men and women ought to be a matter of choice, not law. Worst of all, speakers and writers championed a belief that "security is not to be promoted by stifling the voice of discontent, but by removing its cause."

Such advocacies — labeled anarchy — cost the newspaper its mailing privileges and triggered the closure of Home's post office in 1902. Ten years later, a Tacoma jury convicted Home residents of swimming nude, and the editor who dared to print a commentary titled "prudes *versus* nudes" went to jail for two months.

Today, back-to-the-land movements readily take root in backwoods corners. Even in our cities, an awareness of frontier lingers. Closets hold ski boots, hiking boots, and hip boots; and anyone blessed with a low enough REI number is likely to mention it as a form of ups-manship. Louis and I have Number 6275, which is moderately prestigious. It identifies us as oldtimers at Recreational Equipment, Inc., the renowned co-op supplier of outdoor equipment which began in Seattle in 1938 and now has numerous far-flung branches. We joined REI in 1952.

King County, with one-third of the state's population, now dickers over shipping its trash to Klickitat County, and state fisheries officials contemplate the wisdom of an upriver ride for salmon trying to spawn in drought-lowered waters. Nuclear submarines berth near Bremerton. Boeing planes circle the globe. Sea-Tac airport — which was new when we first came to the state — must be augmented. Bellevue — where a whaling fleet used to tie up for the winter — now bristles with glassy high-rises that look like Newport Beach, California, somehow moved north. Yet in spite of all this, both *yuppies* and folks in the boondocks dig clams, cut firewood, and fill freezers with venison and wild huckleberries.

My friend Dave Pugh, who is Chief of Interpretation for the northwest region of the National Park Service, moved here recently from the San Francisco Bay area. He points out that much of the sense of space within the Puget Sound megalopolis derives from the merciful screening effect of vegetation. "Cut the trees and we'd all be surprised at how crowded it actually is," he says. I suppose he is right. But — call it youthful confidence or call it mature environmental awareness — we western Washingtonians expect to have both scenery and cities. We belong to the 1990s, but also rejoice in our 1790s scenery.

Lieutenants Puget and Whidbey would notice scattered lights if they were to again spend a night near this cove, but they would also recognize the shore. Time rests gently throughout most of Puget Sound and the lowland river valleys.

Boats to match every purpose are to be found in the San Juans. Purse seiners congregate on the Salmon Banks off Cattle Point on San Juan Island to capture sockeye salmon bound for Fraser River; sailboats, within sight of Mount Baker fifty miles away, thread waters with currents of up to ten knots; cabin cruisers setting out from Victoria, British Columbia, can make island moorages in an hour. Setting ashore is often done in a dinghy. For those without boats of their own, the ferry system facilitates travel to Lopez, Shaw, Orcas, and San Juan islands, where further exploration is often undertaken by foot, bicycle, or automobile.

■*Above:* In the 1850s, Roche Harbor on San Juan Island held a Hudson's Bay Company trading post; in 1890, it was the site of the west's largest lime operation. ■*Right:* Starting in the early 1900s, bulb growing has flourished in the sandy loam soils of western Washington valleys; some are even exported to Holland.

■*Left:* A Skagit Valley farm produces a high yield of barley where a century earlier oats—to feed draft horses used in the logging and farming industries — was the main crop. ■*Above:* A pea field blooms in the Skagit Valley near Mount Vernon. Cauliflower, potatoes, cabbage seed, bulbs, and blueberries are also grown.

■*Above:* Built for the 1962 Seattle World's Fair, the 605-foot Space Needle is the city's most famous landmark. ■*Right:* Magnolia, situated above Elliott Bay, is only one of Seattle's thirty-plus named neighborhoods. ■*Overleaf:* Home to half a million, Seattle is the most northerly major city in the lower forty-eight states.

Founded in 1861, the University of Washington moved in 1895 to its present site on 680 acres between Lake Washington and Lake Union. A central quad with rows of ornamental cherry trees, surrounded by gothic-style buildings carries a venerable feeling. The University, besides educating over thirty-five thousand students, is a major research institution. The Port of Seattle, with ship terminals on Elliott Bay, serves some forty ocean shipping lines, totaling more than one thousand vessels each year. Giant cranes annually handle one million cargo containers, which travel on land by truck or train. Seattle is the closest U.S. port to Japan.

Water close by, mountains not far, and people from diverse lands — all contribute to the quality of life in Seattle. Stretching more than the length of Seattle, Lake Washington provides an idyllic setting for shore communities including Kirkland, Bellevue, and Mercer Island. Lake Washington, Lake Union, and Green Lake Park offer attractions no matter what one's interests. Activities include jogging, biking, rowing, canoeing, sailing, watching hydroplane races, fishing, or feeding the ducks. Attracted by surroundings similar to their homeland, twenty thousand Scandinavians have chosen to live in Seattle. People from Asian countries — including Japan, Taiwan, Vietnam, Thailand, and the Philippines — also call Seattle home.

■*Above:* Begun in 1907, Pike Place Market offers Yakima melons, Westport crabs, Puget Sound salmon, and more. ■*Right:* Near Boeing Field, Museum of Flight exhibits include an eighteen-passenger 1929 Boeing trimotor. ■*Overleaf:* A hydropower plant has generated electricity at 268-foot Snoqualmie Falls since 1898.

Logs and finished lumber are major export items at Tacoma's Commencement Bay.

Built in 1950, the Tacoma Narrows Bridge connects mainland Tacoma to the Kitsap Peninsula.

At 14,410 feet, Mount Rainier is the highest point in Washington. Captain George Vancouver named the mountain after a British admiral who never laid eyes on it. In 1792, Vancouver described the Puget Sound area as "a landscape almost as enchantingly beautiful as the most elegant pleasure grounds in Europe."

■*Above:* Completed in 1928, the legislative building is the focal point of the state capitol in Olympia. ■*Right:* Quileute Indians fish for smelt in the surf at La Push on the Olympic coast. Their ancestors lived in huge cedar lodges and pursued whales, seals, halibut, salmon, and sea otters in dugout canoes.

■*Left:* Lupine flourishes at the higher elevations in the Olympic Mountains. ■*Above:* In 1890, Hart Lake was visited by the army expedition of Lieutenant Joseph O'Neil. ■*Overleaf:* At 7,965 feet, Mount Olympus—with ice up to nine hundred feet deep on its six glaciers—is the highest peak in the Olympic Mountains.

Near Anderson Pass, 6,417-foot Mount LaCrosse is typical of the roadless interior of Olympic National Park.

Red heather and mountain hemlock trees in the Olympic Mountains are often obscured by summer fog.

From Hurricane Ridge, the high peaks of the Olympics stand above valleys filled with early morning fog.

The Dungeness River surges through a canyon in the Jupiter Hills area of the Olympic Mountains. Lieutenant Joseph P. O'Neil and his party of men and mules came within a few miles of this spot in 1885. Prior to that time, only the edges of the Olympic Mountains were known, and O'Neil hoped to find mineral wealth there.

■*Above:* Nourished by particles in the air, moss, fern, and club moss thrive in profusion on bigleaf maple in the moist Hoh River Valley, which receives up to 140 inches of precipitation per year.
■*Right:* At Point of the Arches south of Cape Flattery, sea stacks stand above slabs of upturned sedimentary rock.

■*Left:* As the tide goes out, gulls rest on a rock at Ruby Beach.
■*Above:* Black-tailed deer and tiger lilies, fields of avalanche lilies and wilderness beaches — these and more make up the fourteen hundred-square-mile Olympic National Park, originally set aside in 1909 as Mount Olympus National Monument.

Seeds planted near the end of May yield pumpkins in October on a farm northwest of Centralia. Along with sunny, mild summer weather, clay loam soil deposited by the Chehalis River provides good growing conditions for cucumbers, green beans, carrots, peas, sweet corn, cauliflower, broccoli and pumpkins.

Built in 1889, Port Townsend's Starrett House is an outstanding example of Victorian architecture.

Willapa Bay has exported oysters since the 1850s gold rush when they were transported by schooner to San Francisco.

Dependable summer winds make Long Beach an ideal location for the International Kite Festival.

North Head Lighthouse was built in 1898 in response to shipwrecks at nearby Long Beach.

■*Above:* Western sandpipers doze after feeding on the mudflats of Bowerman Basin near Hoquiam. A million shorebirds stop each spring en route from Latin America to Alaska. ■*Overleaf:* In the early 1900s, Finns established dairy farms and logging operations along Deep River, a slough of the lower Columbia.

■*Left:* Before the dams, a large salmon canning industry existed on the lower Columbia River. Sail-powered gillnet boats kept the Altoona cannery supplied with fresh fish. ■*Above:* Bright spring Chinook salmon are a favorite delicacy in Northwest cuisine.

The Columbian white-tailed deer, once abundant, is now an endangered species due to loss of suitable habitat.

Cathlamet was established in 1846 when a retired employee of the Hudson's Bay Company set up a trading post near the end of the Columbia River's twelve hundred-mile journey. Today, the town is supported by logging, dairy farms, and a marina.

■*Above:* Over eight hundred fishing vessels — some working in Alaskan waters — call Grays Harbor home and make necessary repairs there. ■*Right:* Bigleaf maple, important in furniture and cabinetmaking today, was used by Northwest Coast Indians to make bowls, cradle boards, and canoe paddles.

Above: Vancouver, Washington, which was founded in 1825 as Fort Vancouver, was part of Hudson's Bay Company's fur trading empire. In 1873, Mother Joseph brought the House of Providence to Vancouver. *Right:* Clark County surrounding Vancouver still retains some of its rural character.

Of Washington's volcanic giants, 10,436-foot Glacier Peak is considered least likely to erupt in the near future.

THE MOUNTAIN SPINE

We moved to Mount Rainier in the early 1950s, transferred by the National Park Service from Death Valley and the tall cactus country of the Mexican borderlands. The van driver who brought our goods commented: "You've moved from the ridiculous to the sublime."

And sublime it was—although for two weeks the mountain stayed hidden within clouds, and even where to look for it puzzled me. The kids, ages five and seven, immediately set out exploring and soon reported back astonished: "There's *nothing* poisonous here." No rattlesnakes or scorpions, no cactus thorns. Nonetheless, at first I worried that the boys might get lost while playing in the forest. In the desert, no vegetation had blocked their view back to the house.

Funny things happened. A man came to the ranger station and asked to borrow a skillet. When I asked if they had forgotten theirs, he answered, "No. We have it but the campfire would get it dirty." Once, tourists pressed their noses against our windows and exclaimed: "Look. There are people in there!" And a woman getting off a bus asked to use our bathroom because she would feel embarrassed to be seen walking to the public restrooms.

Raccoons and spotted skunks lived under the floor of the house and sometimes fought, a bit odorous for us all. Bats roosted in the wall of our bedroom, and the first couple of nights, Louis thought their odd sounds were me snoring—and I thought they were him snoring. Bears raided the garbage can. One was experienced enough to sit beside the can, straddle it with his hind legs, then tip it gently and slide off the lid. That avoided the clatter he had learned would bring someone to shoo him away.

For a while, a young buck deer tried to join the family. Someone (wrongly) must have taken him from the wild as a fawn, then brought him back when antlers started to appear. More acquainted with people than with other deer, the buck would come onto the porch and whine on cold, rainy days. He enjoyed riding in the cab of the snowplow and tried repeatedly to board the school bus. Twice, he managed to get on the bus, but he ate sandwiches out of lunch bags and turned himself from a novelty into an enemy.

One day the deer walked into the office and ate the remittance forms used for transferring park entrance fees to the Federal Reserve Bank. That was the end. Arrangements were made to move him to the fenced land at Dupont, a dynamite-manufacturing site near Tacoma. Soon we heard that workmen there were finding lunch bags ripped open, and we knew someone else had left a door open.

Rainier is the tallest of Washington's many peaks. To check the height, volunteers from the U.S. Army Corps of Engineers and the Land Surveyors Association of Washington in 1988 carried equipment to the summit for a re-measurement. They recorded signals from satellites, the first use of modern celestial technology for assessing a terrestrial peak. Announcement of their results, accurate within inches, is scheduled for release during the state's Centennial celebration, eighty years after the first measurement.

That first assessment, in 1909, placed its height at 14,150 feet. Four years later, this changed to 14,408. In 1956, the mountain "grew" two more feet to 14,410. More telling, however, than the changing figures is that although Mount Rainier ranks fifth in height among the peaks of the lower forty-eight states, it is the highest of all above its immediate base. Longmire's elevation is only 2,760 feet, whereas the highest peak, Mount Whitney, California — which is 14,495 feet above sea level—and the peaks of the Colorado Rockies start from land already a mile high.

We lived at Rainier when the 1956 measurement was made. It involved lifting U.S. Geological Survey men and triangulation equipment to the summit by helicopter. The pilot did not want to go; the thin air at such an extreme elevation posed a real hazard for a helicopter. He insisted that the doors be taken off and the battery removed after he started the rotor — anything to lighten the load. Then he carried surveyors and equipment up, and later brought the men down. But he refused to go back for the equipment.

Consequently, my husband and another ranger climbed the mountain to bring off the gear and install the new benchmark. I got to go along. On our backs, we carried cement and also gasoline to use as fuel for melting ice, which was needed to mix the cement into concrete for use around the benchmark. In my journal, I noted:

At 1:00 a.m. we left Camp Muir, the traditional 10,000-foot base camp for summit climbs. No moon, so we used headlamps. I was tired, and moving through the darkness seemed like having on a huge hat with the brim hanging down.

Before dawn, the "blinders" effect started to ease. Irregularities in the snow surface cast enough shadow to give texture to the otherwise black world. Then a faintly bright streak lined the eastern horizon. Next—at last—pink light hit the summit and slid down the glacier to warm us. It seemed awfully long in coming.

The new benchmark is located at the high point along the northern rim of the summit crater. Just inside the rim, the ground is free of snow and ice. In fact, it's too hot to sit on.

We Washingtonians feel a connection with the mountain spine dividing us into east and west. We *see* our peaks while going about daily rounds. The Wenatchee Mountains rise beyond the wheat fields of the Waterville Plateau. Mount Adams shows from Yakima. Mount Rainier dots the horizon as you drive toward Ellensburg from Vantage, and it looms huge as you roll along I-5 between Seattle and Olympia. Mount Baker and the North Cascades back-drop the tulip fields of the Skagit River delta. And of course there is Mount St. Helens. St. Helens that we almost hoped would erupt—until it did so and became a two-year nuisance. St. Helens that still evokes the question, Where were you when the mountain blew?

Snowking Lake in the Glacier Peak Wilderness owes its color to pulverized rock particles washed from a nearby glacier.

Water droplets catch on tiny hairs on the leaves of lupine — a plant common in Washington mountains.

In Tacoma, the May 18, 1980, eruption did little except turn the eastern sky murky and fill television screens with images of the Toutle River pouring water from suddenly melted glaciers against the I-5 bridge. Later, lesser eruptions dusted our petunias with ash and turned the keyboard of my electric typewriter gritty when I forgot to cover it.

Even eastern Washingtonians who lived through the darkness-at-noon trauma and the heavy shoveling of fallout from the initial eruption grew weary, most of all, from what seemed like endless small effects. "I'm so tired of sand between my toes when the nearest beach is two hundred miles away," a woman living in the Ahtanum Valley near Yakima told us. "Why do geologists speak of volcanic *ash*? It's *sand*."

I have read that the May 18 eruption equaled the force of thirty atomic bombs dropped at Hiroshima, and also that it equated with five hundred atomic bombs. Either way, mighty though it was, the St. Helens blast was puny, even among other Northwest volcanic eruptions. Mount Mazama, Oregon, ejected nine and one-half cubic miles of debris when it formed Crater Lake and dusted Washington with ash nearly seven thousand years ago. Archaeologists readily recognize this ash within excavation walls and use it as a time marker: anything lying undisturbed above the ash is more recent than the eruption; anything below it is older. They also use ash from previous St. Helens eruptions. The most recent major eruption of Mount St. Helens spewed barely one-quarter cubic mile of ejecta — useful for future archaeologists, but modest compared to Mount Mazama's greatest blast.

Perhaps what the 1980 eruption did above all else was remind us that "dormant" is not "dead." Our human time scale, imbued with an awareness of individual life spans, gives a poor sense of nature's schedules. St. Helens had not erupted for a century. To most of us, but not to scientists, that had seemed to lessen the probability of eruption. Not so.

If I were to pick a favorite mountain drive, it would be to Harts Pass, above the town of Winthrop (which is known more for its Hollywood-frontier atmosphere than for its actual late 1800s role as supply point for ranchers and miners). I like the Harts Pass Road—narrow, rough, and unpaved—because it claws its way into the mountains. Meet an oncoming car, and one of you must back. You hug contours rather than conquer them, as is true while driving the smooth ribbon of the North Cascades Highway.

A short way beyond 6,197-foot Harts Pass, the highest point in the state reached by road, a fire lookout tops Slate Peak. From it, you gaze southeast to scores of peaks gouged into fangs by glacier ice. These include The Needles and Liberty Bell, which tower above the North Cascades Highway. Forty-six miles westward from Slate Peak is the icy-white lump of Mount Baker. Northward is the Pasayten Wilderness. Standing in the absolute midst of *mountain-ness,* you might feel guilty for having won the experience with tires instead of boots except for the exhilaration of beholding such beauty.

I always marvel at the indomitable spirit of the miners who penetrated this realm, which is more vertical than horizontal. In the 1890s, they used horses to pack in a steam-powered stampmill; then they packed out gold for shipment down the Columbia River via stern-wheeler. In the 1900s, they upgraded the old horse trail into a road wide enough for trucks with eighteen inches cut from their axles. Winter contact with the outside world was by dogsled, a scheduled service that brought in mail, urgent supplies, and a motion picture, and took out mail and gold bullion.

A recent issue of *Okanogan Heritage,* a county historical society quarterly, printed a 1935 letter from a miner at the Azurite Mine to his wife:

> We had a long cold spell, 29 below and froze our water pipe up and we have to carry our water from the creek up hill through the deep snow.... It turned warm and started to snow. I never saw anything like it—seven feet in two days. It then started to rain and poured down for three days. The old snow was packed hard and conditions were just right for snowslides.
>
> They started at once and hell was popping for five days. There was hardly a five-minute interval that you couldn't see a slide running in the daytime or hear one roar at night. Some of the big ones filled the air with snow so you could hardly see.

Buildings got knocked down, and the roof of the sawmill caved in from snow load. An avalanche buried the bull cook, but rescuers dug him free within an hour. "We are having wonderful, mild clear weather now," the letter concludes, "but when the next heavy snow comes there will be some nervous men here."

Mining began in the Okanogan Cascades in the 1860s when prospectors who had rushed to the gold boom along the Fraser River in British Columbia returned south with their pockets still empty. Some even say that as early as 1846, surveyors determining the international boundary noticed gold in the Similkameen River and did some panning.

The first claims were for placer gold washed down from the mountains over the millennia. It settled into the sand and gravel of streams and rivers and left shiny flecks and nuggets that miners collected by swirling water in pans or in "rockers," boxes that were filled with gravel and water, then tilted back and forth to catch gold against built-in baffles. White men often worked such claims and moved on. Chinese miners then took over and, with infinite patience, succeeded where get-rich-quick impulses had failed. Ditches dug by the Chinese to divert water for gold operations also irrigated vegetable gardens, the first of the vast systems that now have replaced sagebrush and greasewood with orchards and fields.

Hardrock mining came next. Its evidence still dots the mountains with an odd legacy of leftovers, for following veins into the earth itself required machinery, and that required a capital outlay undreamed of by the placer miners. That investment of capital, in turn, offered its own new possibilities of wealth—with or without ore.

At the Monte Cristo mine (up the Stillaguamish drainage from Everett), the J. D. Rockefeller syndicate invested three million dollars and got a return on its money. Conversely, east of the mountains, the Palmer Mountain Tunnel and Power Company floated stock, blasted a mile-long tunnel, and built a concentrating mill near Loomis. The mill's many windows neither lit nor ventilated the conversion of ore into matte, however, for all that actually ever came out of it was the tar and feathering of a newspaperman who wrote about assured profit and jobs. The mill remnants today are a concrete floor three hundred feet long and a truly striking photograph at the Okanogan County Historical Museum.

Scattered pockets of old-growth forest still remain in places untouched by fires or saws.

Using ice axe, rope, and crampons, climbers on Mount Baker's Roosevelt Glacier explore *seracs,* giant chunks of ice.

Another monument to hope — or folly — is the "China Wall." Jonathan Bourne, Jr., the Harvard educated son of a wealthy Massachusetts whaling family, came to the Northwest in 1878. Shipwrecked off Formosa, he met a sea captain acquaintance of his father's who was bringing Chinese laborers to the Northwest, a virtual slave trade dealing in human cargo. Bourne took passage from Hong Kong to Portland, passed the Oregon bar, then spent his energy organizing mining ventures and dabbling in politics rather than practicing law. With investment money from fellow members of Portland's aristocratic Arlington Club, he bought claims south of Conconully and organized a mining company named for the club. There he built the foundation for a huge mill: the China Wall.

A few summers ago, we turned off the Loop Loop Pass Road to find the mill site. We wound up a narrow valley, unsure of the precise location but knowing what to watch for. Actualities surprised us. Walls stand nearly obscured by Douglas fir and larch. They would be easy to pass without noticing, yet a single section bulks fully thirty feet high and eighty feet long. No Chinese ever were associated with Bourne's company; the nickname China Wall comes from its built-for-eternity character. A stonemason named Chris Starzman who had homesteaded near Brewster directed the work. Among those under him were Antoire Ritchie, a Frenchman from Canada who lived in the valley nearby (the ruins of his cabin still stand); John Bawlf, a Civil War veteran who had crossed the Great Plains to Coulee City by wagon train; and Robert Saltmarsh, a wheat farmer from Almira who worked on the wall to earn cash.

Somehow Starzman got these men and scores of others equally inexperienced to build walls fit for an imperial palace. Three to four feet thick, corners incorporating blocks of granite as great as 4 by 2 by 1 feet, the walls rise in nearly a dozen courses, base for the various levels of the expected mill. They are aesthetically and functionally perfect — or would have been functional, had the mill been finished. But it was not. Freighters brought equipment, including two three-ton boilers, into the little valley, a feat in itself; tens of thousands of bricks were manufactured and delivered; and huge squared timbers were hewn. But fate decreed that no complete superstructure should rise from the magnificent foundation. Bourne began work on the mill in August 1889, ordered a stop in May 1890. His Arlington Club investors had tired of pouring money into the ground, getting none back out.

Obviously, all who live among mountains experience their moods, but in Washington, lowlanders also are affected. We watch the peaks dress and undress seasonally and know that the world is white as well as blue and green. Snowfall at Paradise, a mile-high shoulder of Mount Rainier, has logged a record 1,027 inches of snow. That amounts to eighty-five *feet*. It settles into a blanket so deep that winter access to back-country cabins comes only by digging *down* to second-story windows, and often well into July, guests enter Paradise Inn through a snow tunnel.

By then, avalanche lilies herald a parade of bloom so wondrous that if rainbows were on the ground instead of among the clouds, alpen meadows would surely be their home. Soon, flakes float from the sky, and the mountains regain their white robe. Skiers rejoice. In Washington, ours is more than a poetic passion for mountains. We actively pursue their delights.

■*Preceding page:* Beneath American Border and Canadian Border peaks, Tomyhoi Lake reflects light from the surrounding mountainsides. ■*Above:* Unlike neighboring Mount Baker, 9,127-foot Mount Shuksan is not volcanic in origin. ■*Right:* Golden alpine larch is common near Harts Pass, elevation 6,197 feet.

■*Left:* Pink bouquets of Lewis monkeyflower are common in the Cascades wherever water seeps out of the ground. ■*Above:* Meaning "the great white watcher," *Kulshan* is the Indian name for 10,778-foot Mount Baker. Twenty square miles of glaciers covering the mountain's slopes add credibility to the name.

Goat Flats, at 4,700 feet, is part of the Cascade Range uplift that began ten million years ago. Fourteen thousand years ago glaciers carved out the Puget Sound region to the west of the Cascades. Today, Orcas Island lies sixty miles northwest of Goat Flats.

In the Glacier Peak Wilderness, 6,400-foot Little Giant Pass is a hikers' passage to the Napeequa River.

Chiwawa Mountain is reflected in a shallow sedge-filled pond beside Lyman Lake in the Glacier Peak Wilderness.

Morning and evening sunlight often creates pink highlights, called alpenglow, on 10,778-foot Mount Baker. A sleeping giant, Mount Baker has erupted several times since the last ice age. The most recent major activity was a venting of ash and steam, called fumarolic, which occurred in 1975.

■*Above:* Lake Chelan, fifty-one miles long and 1,529 feet deep, fills a glacier-carved valley. ■*Right:* Rocky Mountain maple and red osier dogwood create fall color along Buttermilk Creek near Twisp. ■*Overleaf:* East of Marblemount in the North Cascades National Park, Eldorado Peak stands at 8,868 feet.

Summers are brief in the North Cascades due to a combination of latitude and elevation. Lakes and ponds may remain frozen into August or later. Wildflowers must grow, bloom, and set seed in the brief period following snow melt and before the ground becomes too dry. Although snow flurries may occur in any month, winter sets in to stay in November, and the North Cascades becomes a vast wilderness untracked by man but inhabited by mountain goats, snowshoe hares, gray jays, spruce grouse, ptarmigan, and lynx.

The Skykomish River offers wild rafting rides. Each summer week-
end city dwellers head for the mountains to hike, climb, kayak,
fish, camp, and enjoy nature. In winter, several alpine ski areas
provide recreation in the Cascades. Cross-country skiers choose
from frozen lakes, meadows, and logging roads.

Top Lake north of Stevens Pass is a stop on the Pacific Crest Trail that runs from Canada to Mexico.

Mount Stuart, 9,415 feet, cuts a jagged outline above Windy Pass on the drier east slope of the Cascades.

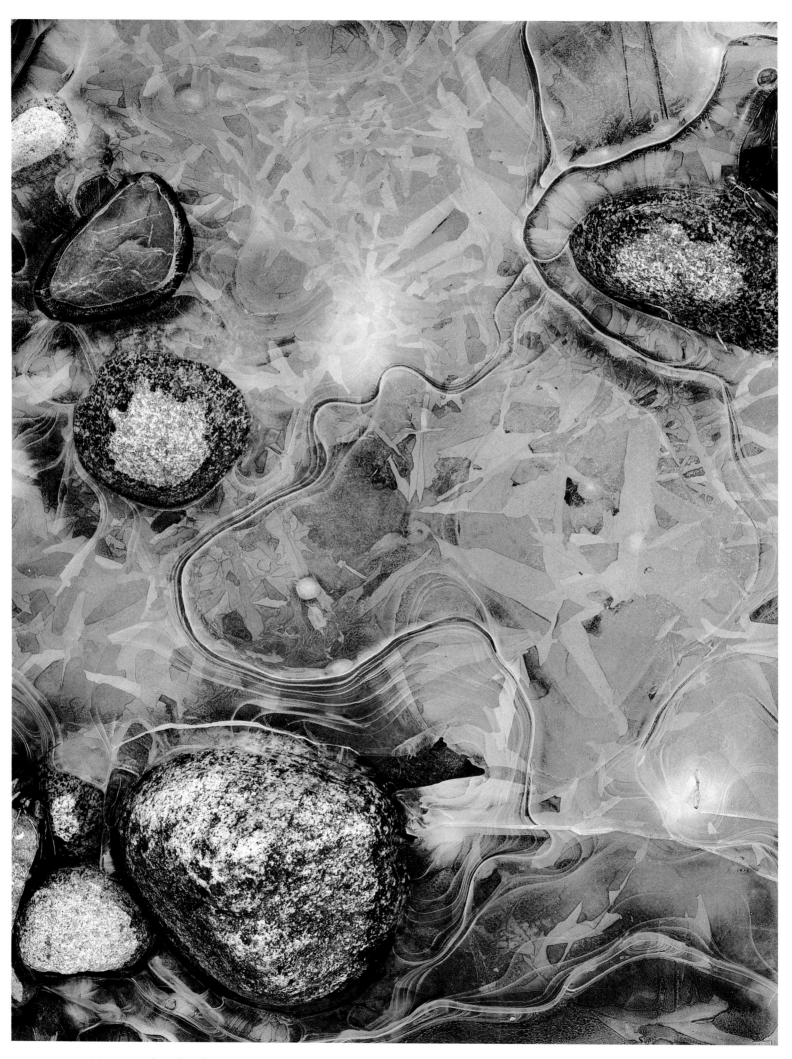

Air trapped under the ice creates interesting patterns when Icicle Creek's flow drops during a cold snap.

The tunnel near Cayuse Pass in Mount Rainier National Park is a fine example of 1930s stone masonry.

Spectacle Lake fills a depression scoured out of granite by a glacier in the headwaters of the Cle Elum River. It is one of seven hundred lakes in the three hundred ninety-three thousand-acre Alpine Lakes Wilderness east of Seattle. The area received official protection with the signature of President Gerald Ford in 1976.

Forty-eight species of the brightly colored Indian paintbrush grow in a variety of habitats throughout the Northwest, spread from sea coast to mountain top to desert. At least one subspecies is found on Cockscomb Mountain south of Mount Rainier National Park in the Gifford Pinchot National Forest.

Mount Index, 5,979 feet, rises abruptly from its five hundred-foot base elevation along the Skykomish River.

More common on western slopes of the Cascades, vine maple adds color to an eastern slope ponderosa pine stand.

Some ten miles wide at its base, Mount Rainier's heights are covered with thirty-five square miles of glaciers. Established in 1899, Mount Rainier National Park preserves 378 square miles, including mountain lakes, waterfalls, and meadows which support wildlife such as marmots, mountain goats, elk, and birds.

■*Above:* Combined with cold, water seeping from fractured granite results in massive icicles above Icicle Creek. ■*Right:* The South
Fork of the Skykomish River near the town of Index runs clear and
cold. ■*Overleaf:* When the water is calm, Lemah Mountain and
Chimney Rock reflect clearly in Cooper Lake near Cle Elum.

■*Left:* Evidence of a volcanic history, hexagonal columns of andesite lava are found at Mount Rainier National Park. ■*Above:* Leprechaun Lake, one of the Enchantment Lakes in the eastern Cascades, exemplifies the "enchantment" part of the name, especially in fall when the alpine larch turns yellow.

The rugged peaks of the Goat Rocks Wilderness form the back-
bone of the Cascades, separating the Tieton and Klickitat river
drainages on the east side from the Cowlitz drainage on the west
side. Mount Rainier looms seventy miles in the distance.

Water from springs around Mount Adams plunges over Lewis River's Upper Falls in the Gifford Pinchot National Forest.

The May 1980 eruption reduced 9,677-foot Mount St. Helens to its present height of 8,366 feet.

Indicating a steady stream flow and an absence of scouring floods, lush moss grows at Twin Falls Creek between Trout Lake and Randle in the Gifford Pinchot National Forest. Glacial water from Mount Adams, traveling beneath lava flows and issuing as springs, is the source of many streams in the area.

■*Above:* A Yakima Indian word, *Wenatchee,* meaning "river issuing from canyon," aptly describes the Wenatchee River in
Tumwater Canyon. ■*Right:* Summit Creek, originating in the
William O. Douglas Wilderness, takes a last plunge before joining
the Ohanapecosh River near Mount Rainier National Park.

■*Left:* On the day following a winter storm, the trees around the Goat Rocks and Mount Adams appear ghostlike with their mantle of snow. ■*Above:* The Goat Rocks, an extinct volcano located between Mounts Rainier and Adams, are visible from Hogback Mountain, south of White Pass.

At 12,276 feet, Mount Adams is Washington's second highest peak. Because of its broad shape, Mount Adams is thought to have been built by several volcanoes in close proximity. Described by Lewis and Clark as a "high humped mountain," Adams is named after the second president of the United States.

Wind River, sixty miles east of Vancouver in the Columbia Gorge, lures fly-fishermen casting for summer-run steelhead.

Summer winds running *against* the current make the Columbia River the windsurfing capital of the world.

Arrowleaf balsamroot grows around a fallen oak branch near Lyle in the botanically rich Columbia River Gorge.

Sumac grows throughout the dry hills of eastern Washington, especially in draws where moisture collects.

EASTERN WASHINGTON

Spokane is well nicknamed the Queen City of the Inland Empire. Travel through, and little of the charm is apparent. Pause, and you find it.

"Architecture offers a way to get a handle on Spokane," says Scott Brooks-Miller, Historic Preservation Officer for the city. Then he outlines a tour ranging from buildings in the shape of milk bottles (intended as ice cream parlors) and an automotive repair garage, with an entry that looks like a 1930s car radiator, to storybook mansions in Browne's Addition and on South Hill.

Brooks-Miller — young, knowledgeable, enamored of his work — explains: "Eastern Washington has had three centers: Walla Walla, Colfax, and Spokane. Today, Walla Walla has the state penitentiary and the U.S. Army Corps of Engineers. Colfax has a thousand people more than it did in 1890. And Spokane is where everybody goes — for everything.

"A rail connection to the east came here in 1881 and, about the same time, hardrock miners found first gold, then silver, copper, and lead. That combination of trains and mines gave Spokane its start as an economic center extending from British Columbia and over into Montana clear down to the Snake River and west to the Columbia." With those words, Scott leads me downtown to see what he calls Twenty-year Buildings. He says, "That's how long we expect construction to last these days without needing major repair." He also speaks of One-hundred-year Buildings. "They were built to last, and with modern techniques, we can keep them forever."

By the 1890s, Spokane was beyond the boomtown stage. Building styles and techniques were contemporary with the rest of the United States. Today, pedestrian skywalks link these structures — the "largest and oldest skywalk network in the U.S. except for Minneapolis-St. Paul." In a sense, the enclosed corridors convert most of Spokane's downtown section into a mall; you walk from building to building at the second-story level, yet contend with neither traffic nor wind nor winter snow.

Along two blocks of Stevens Street, Scott showed me buildings representing forty years of change. They stand virtually side by side, an unusual variety of styles from the past yet pleasantly intermixed with modern construction. The earliest buildings were masonry, put up after fire leveled Spokane's mostly wooden downtown in 1889. Cast-iron store fronts replaced the wooden construction, a technique that opened up the street level beyond what was structurally possible with all-masonry walls, which need a thick base as support for upper walls. "Cast-iron store fronts were a real advantage for shops. They let merchants display their wares to the street."

Steel construction followed cast-iron fronts. Buildings rose higher, their walls punctured with windows. The Old National Bank Building is fifteen stories high. It gleams with white terra-cotta, a lightweight cladding that offers infinite possibilities of molding to produce varied textures and shapes. On the Sherwood Building, gargoyles sit above the entry, and stylized gothic arches texture the facade. By the 1920s, Portland cement replaced lime mortar, which is vulnerable to weathering. Concrete could be poured into forms; walls could be raised by setting one pre-formed section on top of another, essentially the same technique as building with stone.

"Soon after that, buildings began to lose human scale," says Scott. "Earlier, there was no question of where the door was. Cornices and crests clearly defined the edges of buildings, and the first couple of floors and the top floor had a lot of ornate detail. Buildings were designed to reflect their owners' place in society, and architects tried to catch the eye and create a give-and-take between building and beholder.

"Now there's more anonymity—maybe with the beginning of a return to pitched roofs and people-oriented space. Maybe we'll recycle styles, although so far architecture has never done that."

Spokane is situated barely north of the rich, rolling hills of the Palouse, a region blessed with deep, moisture-holding soil and spectacular production of wheat, barley, lentils, and dry peas. To be in the Palouse at harvest time in August is to step within a Norman Rockwell painting updated by mechanization but with defined values remaining intact. Neighborliness. Hard work. Family. Good cheer.

We stayed at Tekoa with friends Gene and Evelyn Fletcher who farm 2,700 acres, some of it land Evelyn's father farmed, some of it leased. The harvest had been underway a week. When we arrived, the three Fletcher combines had just finished harvesting a barley field and were moving to a wheat field five miles away. Evelyn pinpointed their location by calling on a VHF radio, using the frequency assigned to the family's farm operation. Each combine has a radio. Each truck has one. So do the family's equipment shop, the cluster of grain storage bins, and the house. The radio helps keep the harvest moving on a nonstop basis. Just call over it to find someone to fix a breakdown, or bring replacement parts, or take a sample of newly cut grain for a moisture test. If there is more than twelve percent moisture, the elevator cannot accept it for storage.

It is 7:00 p.m. We see the combines pass the bins—three green monsters "flagged" fore and aft by trucks. We fall in behind, a parade of winking warning lights traversing a valley at ten mph while the sun drops behind a ridge and suffuses us with a warm gentle light as if coming through stained glass. We watch the combines open up the field of ripe wheat, their twenty-foot reels rotating like paddle wheels on a riverboat, chaff spewing out the rear and creating the distinctive odor of the harvest. The whole year's work hinges on these August days. Evelyn says: "The best sounds in the world are when they start the combines and when they shut them off with nobody hurt, or killed." Palouse hills are steep. Machines occasionally tip over. Furthermore, the gears, conveyor belts, cutters, and augers — all constantly in motion—bring in the harvest but also pose a hazard for the weary humans tending them.

On the Klickitat River, members of the Yakima Indian Nation carry on an ancient tradition of dip netting for salmon.

An Indian pictograph above the Columbia River at Wishram recalls a people who lived in pit houses.

Gene says he is retired. Yet at 10:00 p.m. he comes home after fifteen hours in the fields, and we eat dinner. He laughs: "Oh, I work full-time during spring planting and harvest. But I don't go out to the shop anymore, or make decisions. I leave that to the boys." The "boys" are sons. Jim has a degree in oceanography and a teaching credential from Berkley. When he decided to come back to farming, he studied plant pathology and microbiology. David's degree is in business administration. He returned to the Palouse after working for Dunn and Bradstreet.

We talk about crops. This year the Fletchers have planted a new variety of wheat, and Gene says it looks promising. "You could hardly fit in another ten straws per acre." Crops other than wheat? "The boys played with lupine; oil from the seeds goes into margarine. It didn't grow well though, and we're too far from the processing plant anyway. Rapeseed for margarine didn't work out either. Farmers here were planting two kinds and they'd hybridize. But the cross wasn't any good."

Lentils have a happier story. Seventh-day Adventists at Farmington, the next town south of Tekoa, grew them years ago because of their high protein content; many Adventists eat no meat. By the 1950s, farmers in the surrounding area also grew lentils. Today ninety percent of the American crop comes from this region.

I ride a combine with Gene harvesting a wheat field. Automatic levelers keep the cab from tilting as we contour hills cutting, gathering, threshing, sorting, and—ultimately—transferring the crop from holding tank to dump truck summoned alongside by radio. Air conditioning saves broiling in the sun. Computer readouts monitor everything from the rate of movement over the ground (averaging one mph while I was aboard) to a malfunction of the chopper or conveyor or half-a-dozen other systems, or an excess of grain blowing out onto the ground with the chaff. The reel turns. The grain heads seem to surge into the header. We circle, empty into the truck, circle again. At dusk Gene turns on lights. Keep rolling. Get in the crop. And if your neighbor is sick, get in his too.

I ride with David harvesting windrows of lentils already swathed and left to cure. It is a dirtier job than cutting wheat. The plants grow only a foot high and the lifters must run along the ground. Dust flies along with chaff. David's left hand steers, his right hand constantly plays a lever adjusting the height of the lifters and header. Abruptly he stops; climbs out with engine running and reel spinning; returns with a rock half the size of a Frisbee. "Hit one of these and you've trashed a $4,000 to $5,000 bar," he explains. Riding in the truck to the storage bin with David's son Jonathan, a senior in computer science at Washington State University, I note how intense the lentils operation is, and Jonathan agrees that his dad is more tired after a day of lentils than of wheat.

Gene told me he did not want the backbreaking work of farming as he knew it while growing up. Then he adds, "But with all this mechanization, why it's fun." That "fun" involves a capital outlay of $160,000 in replacement cost per combine and $90,000 per tractor. Three or four weeks of harvest make you or break you, depending on the weather and the market. In return, the farmer gets about one cent per loaf of bread, less than goes for the plastic wrapper. But satisfaction is deeper than economics. For Palouse farmers it comes from participating in the aesthetics of the land: voluptuous hills stretched to the horizon — and you are tending them, patterning them, knowing their every light and temperature, belonging to their life.

West of the Palouse, the topography roughens. Ice-age floods repeatedly stripped the land to bedrock and plucked at the joints within basalt flows. The result is a maze of canyons (known by the French word *coulees*) cut into a broad sagebrush plateau. Irrigation water from the Columbia Basin Project now makes much of the land green, but long before that, men tried turning sweat into dryland farms. Among these hardworking optimists were — and are — the McGregors, a family whose multi-generation enterprise has evolved through a century. It began with sheep production and went on to range cattle, orchards, experimental irrigation, feed lots, meat packing, and chemical fertilizers.

In Hooper, we met Alex McGregor, author of the book *Counting Sheep*, which chronicles family events from sheepherding days to agri-business. With a doctorate in history, Alex formerly taught at Whitman College in Walla Walla but left to manage the fertilizer division of the McGregor Company. "I wanted the business to survive as a matter of continuity, if nothing else," he says. "And since everybody in my generation was busy with other things, I switched."

We sit at the kitchen table of the comfortable two-story house where Alex was raised. He and his family recently moved to be near the main office in Colfax; previously he was commuting ninety miles a day. (Alex describes Hooper as "equally inconvenient to everywhere.") The greatest sense of "home" still is here, however, and the family returns at every opportunity. The house is one of the fourteen that constitute the entire town along with a store building (now vacant except for a ranch headquarters office), a company hotel/boarding house presently used only for community potlucks and quilting bees, an operating post office with the original oak boxes still in place, and the old wool and sacked-wheat warehouses standing intact by the railroad track. Hooper differs from scores of other pinprick towns in eastern Washington in that it is a company town that has been lived in by three generations of owners as well as employees. The founders were four Scotch brothers who immigrated here from eastern Canada in 1882 and built the business through diligence and thrift.

"We hated to close the store," Alex says, "but when the highway moved across the valley, there weren't enough customers left. Keeping a school got to be a problem too. Over the years, the district consolidated twelve small schools into the one at LaCrosse — and even there the high school next year will have only thirty-five kids."

McGregor Land and Livestock Company no longer raises sheep. Alex explains, "With sheep, you have to do ten things at once — everything from vaccinate the dogs to arrange for a shearing crew. Sheep are labor intensive, and agriculture has moved to mechanization." Basque herders from northern Spain cared for most Columbia Plateau flocks when Alex was growing up. He remembers their diligence and devotion. In his book he tells of asking the foreman, Clemente Barber, about the health of a certain ewe belonging to a band of three thousand sheep. Barber recognized her and recited her life history beginning with abandonment as a lamb, on to the present. "Twice [last year] I pull her out of mud holes to save her," he concluded.

Hispanics pick the majority of Washington's fruit, often working for the same grower year after year.

Grand Coulee Dam, completed in 1942, is the largest concrete structure in the world.

Remembering Barber, Alex laughs about his own first experience driving sheep as a boy. He had learned the right words in Spanish from the Basques, but his inflection was wrong and the dogs absolutely refused to respond. "I sure got tired chasing those sheep by myself," he concludes.

With that, we go to the shearing shed built about 1914, so big it could shelter six thousand ewes in winter although its primary use was for lambing and shearing. Long sacks, weighing three hundred pounds apiece when full of wool, were tamped "by jumping up and down inside the sacks." Behind the shed is a "drop wagon" much like the covered wagons used by westward-bound pioneers but equipped with rubber-tired wheels for pulling behind a pickup truck. Rows of compartments for ewes and newborn lambs line the interior. On the open range, too many lambs fell victim to bad weather or coyotes. Brought in and penned, mothers bond better with their young and give them more care. ("Sheep are smart animals, but they're smart in an unusual way," Alex says. "I'll never admit they're dumb.")

We drive through sagebrush six to eight feet tall and past bunchgrass that in a few months will have a foot of green growth. We picnic across the river from the state park at Palouse Falls (the "big falls," Alex calls them, since there are two other, lesser waterfalls along the Palouse River). These drop 198 feet, the water chocolate brown with soil from Palouse fields. Measurements in the winter of 1962-1963 showed twenty-two million tons of sediment going over the falls, equivalent to 160 acres of soil eighty feet deep. That was the worst year on record. Average erosion is about half of that.

"Soil loss comes from slopes that are pulverized and seeded in September. The plants sprout, then hold dormant through the winter. The ground freezes, and when rains finally come in spring, they can't soak in. We end up with a double loss: the soil erodes and the moisture we need runs off." Then Alex talks about fertilizers and herbicides. Aerial spraying is not precise compared to application made from the ground; spray may blow or get dumped in the wrong place. The McGregors are experimenting with machinery for injecting fertilizer and herbicides—perhaps even combined with seed—directly into the ground through the previous year's stubble. That would eliminate need for tillage; and with stubble still in place, erosion would be controlled. Alex summarizes: "It's gratifying to be a part of agriculture's constant change—a part of history. You go out to your own blacksmith shop and see if you can affect the future."

We drive down a coulee gouged by ice-age floods and stop at a pothole lake, where cottonwoods edge the water. Farther on, we walk to the drop-off into Palouse Canyon and gaze across the Snake River country to the Blue Mountains perhaps seventy miles to the south.

We revel in the scene, then return to Hooper. Alex's kids are waiting to take Fig Newtons to a band of half-a-dozen sheep kept as a family symbol. Perhaps it is our unfamiliar truck that sends the sheep running. Eight-year-old Ian predicts, "They'll come when Mom charms them." But they refuse, even though Linda pursues with hand and cookie outstretched. Kate, a pragmatist at age four, says: "Forget it, sheep."

We all leave, the McGregors to return to Pullman, Louis and I to Tacoma. Our route cross-sections Washington geography: vast plateau, river artery, mountains, forestlands, inland waterway. Enchanting variety.

■*Above:* Ten to twelve inches of annual precipitation in the area around Waterville results in yields of thirty to forty bushels of wheat per acre. ■*Right:* While ponderosa pine is predominant, aspen gives colorful variety to the forest in the mountainous northeast part of the state near Colville.

The Columbia Plateau of eastern Washington was shaped first by lava flows, then by ice age floods, and finally by agriculture. Precipitation in some areas averages a mere seven inches. Depending on the path of the ancient Spokane floods which gouged out the Grand Coulee and deposited rich silt elsewhere, soils vary from excellent to poor. Dryland farming is the rule except in the central basin where water diverted from the Columbia River at Grand Coulee Dam is delivered to farmers' fields by a vast system of canals and storage reservoirs that double as recreation areas.

■*Left:* Even today, the tepee has both mystique and practicality. ■*Above:* The Pasayten Wilderness occupies a half million acres east of the North Cascades. ■*Overleaf:* During winter low flow, snow covers cobbles of the Wenatchee River where whitefish and steelhead lurk under the surface—food for eagles and otter.

■*Left:* Fall comes to a peach orchard near Wenatchee. ■*Above:* Harvest over, an orchard near Cashmere awaits pruning, as horses enjoy the last green grass before winter snow. A great many pears, in addition to Washington's famous apples, are grown in the Cashmere-Peshastin-Leavenworth area.

The Wenatchee River provides irrigation water for a major fruit industry which began in 1901 with rail shipment of the first car-load of apples from Wenatchee. In the 1860s, the river corridor was a route for miners traveling from Puget Sound across the Cascades and on to the gold fields of British Columbia.

Lupine adds a touch of blue to a profusion of arrowleaf balsamroot growing on a hillside near Cashmere.

Geography has set the stage for eastern Washington to be a world-class fruit-growing region: Irrigation water is available from both mountain streams and the Columbia River; humidity is low; and nights are cool as harvest approaches. Thirty million apple trees here supply half the fresh-apple market in the country, plus exports to countries as diverse as Hong Kong and Saudi Arabia. Twenty varieties of apples are commonly produced, but Red Delicious predominates. Another seven million trees grow apricots, cherries, nectarines, peaches, pears, and plums. As a northern desert, eastern Washington provides unique conditions for growing wine grapes. Growers control the moisture the vines receive to produce high-quality grapes.

■*Left:* In the remote southeast corner of Washington, the Grande Ronde River flows through a two thousand-foot deep canyon cut through multiple layers of lava rock. ■*Above:* In true western tradition, Blue Mountain cowboys ride the high country near Dayton, searching for strays as winter approaches.

The Touchet River flows out of the Blue Mountains east of Walla Walla. Lava from these mountains covered vast areas of eastern Washington. "Touchet" is an adaptation of the Indian word *tousa,* meaning "curing salmon before a fire."

Built in 1905, this Methodist church stands alone at Rocklyn in the wheat country near Davenport.

Grain elevators form the skyline of the tiny town of St. John in the heart of the Palouse Hills wheat country.

Four thousand square miles of the Palouse Hills spread out below Steptoe Butte near the Idaho border. Windblown soil, called *loess*, along with twenty inches of precipitation, results in wheat yields of sixty to one hundred bushels per acre. Palouse Indians defeated Lieutenant Colonel Edward Steptoe near here in 1857.

■*Above:* As an erosion control measure west of Spokane, strips of wheat alternate with fallow ground. ■*Right:* Spokane County Courthouse was built in 1895. ■*Overleaf:* Falls on the Spokane River played a significant role for the first hydroelectric plant west of the Mississippi and as an attraction at Expo '74.

■*Left:* The Review Building, built in 1891, remains from Spokane's "Age of Elegance," a time of prosperity brought by mining and the location of railroads. ■*Above:* Cottonwood trees reflect in deep Sullivan Lake north of Spokane near Metaline Falls.

■*Above:* A mountain meadow near Smackout Pass in the Colville National Forest provides good summer range for cattle. ■*Right:* A backyard apple tree gone wild brightens a vacant lot in the tiny town of Ione, along the Pend Oreille River north of Spokane.

■*Left:* The Kettle River loops in and out of British Columbia before joining the Columbia River at Kettle Falls. ■*Above:* A hillside of western larch, also known as tamarack, puts on a brilliant fall display in the Colville National Forest east of the town of Republic. The needles of this conifer tree are shed annually.